The Art of War
Interpreted for Entrepreneurs

Ancient Strategic Principles for Building, Defending, and Scaling a Business

ANCIENT WISDOM HACKS

Publisher: NX Inc

Third Edition

Table of Contents

Chapter 8: Leadership That Commands Loyalty and Action
Creating a mission, building trust, and leading through uncertainty

Chapter 9: Adapt or Die
Pivoting with discipline, listening deeply, and evolving ahead of threats

Chapter 10: Victory Without Complacency
Sustaining success, avoiding drift, and building for long-term resilience

Conclusion: The War Never Ends—And That's the Point
Strategy as mindset, leadership as craft, and the founder as field commander

Introduction: War, Business, and the Game of Survival

Why *The Art of War* Still Matters

Over two thousand years ago, a Chinese general named Sun Tzu wrote a series of concise, hard-hitting lessons on warfare that would outlive empires, dynasties, and revolutions. His book, *The Art of War*, has been studied by military leaders, corporate executives, athletes, and politicians for one simple reason: it is not really about war.

It is about strategy. About outthinking your opponents, understanding your environment, managing people, and winning with minimal loss. Strip away the ancient language, and *The Art of War* becomes a blueprint for navigating high-stakes environments where resources are tight, competition is fierce, and the cost of mistakes is high. If that doesn't sound like the daily life of an entrepreneur, nothing does.

"If you know the enemy and know yourself, you need not fear the result of a hundred battles," Sun Tzu wrote. For founders, this means deeply understanding their own capabilities, market position, and internal culture, as well as knowing their customers, competitors, and industry shifts. Those who master this dual awareness don't just survive—they dominate.

This book still matters because the fundamentals of strategic advantage haven't changed. Whether you're commanding battalions or bootstrapping a SaaS startup, you win by seeing what others don't, moving faster than your rivals, and deploying your resources where they count most. Sun Tzu's writing is timeless not because it talks about swords and horses, but because it drills into the essence of intelligent action.

Entrepreneurship as Modern Warfare: Limited Resources, Shifting Terrain, Relentless Competition

Starting and growing a business today is an act of war by another name. You face entrenched competitors, limited cash flow, volatile markets, technological upheaval, and the pressure to adapt or perish. There are no maps, no rules, no guarantees. Only the terrain in front of you, and how well you read and respond to it.

Sun Tzu wrote, "In the midst of chaos, there is also opportunity." Entrepreneurs must operate with that mindset. The chaos of modern business—supply chain breakdowns, platform changes, new regulations, viral competitors—is not a signal to retreat. It is the playing field. Those who thrive are not those who demand stability, but those who train themselves to maneuver within instability.

Startups are fundamentally outnumbered and outgunned. They can't match the war chests of Big Tech or the infrastructure of legacy corporations. Yet again and again, they win. Why? Because they are agile. Because they strike quickly. Because they don't waste resources fighting unwinnable battles. As Sun Tzu puts it, "The skillful fighter puts himself into a position which makes defeat impossible, and does not miss the moment for defeating the enemy."

Modern entrepreneurs face asymmetric warfare. It's not a question of who has more, but who uses what they have more strategically. Just as guerrilla fighters use terrain, timing, and intelligence to counter larger forces, smart startups exploit speed, focus, and customer insight to punch above their weight.

Shifting terrain is a constant. Market conditions evolve. Customer preferences pivot. Algorithms change overnight. Entire industries can be reshaped in months. "Water shapes its course according to the nature of the ground over which it flows," Sun Tzu observed. The best entrepreneurs do the same: they remain fluid, adjusting their strategies to the reality around them, never married to a fixed plan.

And then there's the competition. Relentless. Fast-following. Often better funded. The entrepreneur's job isn't just to be better—it's to be different. To act in ways that force others to respond. "To move swiftly, strike vigorously, and secure the objective before the enemy has time to react" is as true for launching a new feature as it was for laying siege to a city.

Entrepreneurship isn't a romantic journey. It's tactical. It demands sacrifice, grit, misdirection, and momentum. It is war.

How This Book Works: From Sun Tzu's Maxims to Entrepreneurial Moves

The Art of War is often quoted, rarely applied. Its beauty lies in its simplicity. But turning it into business strategy takes more than pulling out aphorisms. It requires translation—from maxims to moves.

That's what this book does. Each chapter takes a core principle from *The Art of War* and reframes it in the language of entrepreneurship. No swords, no armor, no generals. Just actionable strategy for founders trying to build, scale, and survive.

You'll learn how to:

- Position your startup before competitors even realize you're a threat.

- Build an organization that thrives in uncertainty.

- Recognize terrain changes before others do.

- Execute quickly while preserving flexibility.

- Use perception as a force multiplier.

- Lead with clarity, not charisma.

- Avoid battles you can't win, and win without fighting when possible.

Each chapter starts with Sun Tzu's principle, then breaks it down into tactical questions and practical frameworks you can use immediately. This is not about theory. It's about fighting smart in the real world.

Because at the end of the day, business is not just a game. It's a contest of will, clarity, and endurance. The winners are those who think several moves ahead, prepare in silence, and strike with precision.

Sun Tzu taught how to win without needless conflict. This book shows entrepreneurs how to build with the same level of cunning, discipline, and strategic foresight. Welcome to your war room.

Chapter 1: Know Yourself, Know Your Market

"If you know the enemy and know yourself, you need not fear the result of a hundred battles." — Sun Tzu

Introduction: The Most Important Battle

Before you build your product, raise capital, or go to market, you must win two foundational battles: one internal and one external. The internal battle is self-awareness—understanding your motivations, strengths, blind spots, and decision-making patterns as a founder. The external battle is understanding your market—your customer, your competition, your ecosystem. This chapter gives you the blueprint to fight and win both.

Sun Tzu doesn't open *The Art of War* with tactics. He starts with philosophy and foundations. His strategy begins with *knowing*—because knowledge is leverage, and in both war and business, leverage is everything.

---

1. Know Yourself: The Psychology of a Founder

"Know yourself and you will win all battles."

You are the general of your company. Your clarity, mindset, and emotional intelligence influence every decision, especially under pressure. Sun Tzu knew that the self could be both an asset and a liability. The same holds true for entrepreneurs.

1.1. What Drives You?

Start with your **motivations**. Are you building for freedom? Status? Impact? Wealth? Ego? Legacy? Understanding your "why" determines your endurance. Motivation becomes your fuel during uncertainty and setbacks, which are inevitable.

Ask yourself:

- Would I still pursue this if no one noticed?

- Am I solving a problem I care about, or chasing validation?

- What outcome would feel like a win—even if it looks like a loss to others?

This is not philosophical fluff—it's strategic grounding. Founders who don't know their motivation build brittle companies.

1.2. Strengths and Weaknesses

"He who knows himself is enlightened." — Lao Tzu

Identify your **core strengths**: Are you a product thinker? A storyteller? An operator? A deal-maker? Double down on them. Then surround yourself with people who offset your weaknesses—not clones of yourself.

Use a **Founder's SWOT**:

- **Strengths**: What do I consistently excel at?

- **Weaknesses**: Where do I slow the team down?

- **Opportunities**: What trends or capabilities can I uniquely leverage?

- **Threats**: What internal patterns sabotage me?

Great generals don't try to be great at everything. They deploy strengths with precision and shield weaknesses through delegation, systems, or partnerships.

1.3. Watch Your Biases

Cognitive biases kill startups quietly. Sun Tzu warned against pride, impulsiveness, and underestimation. Modern founders are equally vulnerable:

- **Confirmation bias**: Ignoring signals that your idea is flawed.

- **Overconfidence**: Scaling before product-market fit.

- **Sunk cost fallacy**: Refusing to pivot due to past investments.

"He who is prudent and lies in wait for an enemy who is not, will be victorious."

Prudence begins with self-checks. Use advisors, co-founders, or even structured journaling to spot and challenge your thinking errors before they become execution errors.

---

2. Know the Market: Reconnaissance Before Battle

"If ignorant both of your enemy and yourself, you are certain to be in peril."

Too many founders treat market research like a checkbox instead of what it truly is: **strategic reconnaissance**. In Sun Tzu's world, war generals sent scouts. In your world, it's about customer interviews, competitor tracking, and intel gathering.

2.1. Customers: Map Their Reality

Your customer is not a persona. They are a real person with pain, context, alternatives, and constraints. Your job is to uncover truth, not validate your assumptions.

Start with:

- What problem do they actually have?

- How are they solving it today?

- What are they frustrated with?

- What language do they use when describing it?

> *"In war, the way is to avoid what is strong and to strike at what is weak."*

You win by attacking unsolved pain points your competitors haven't addressed. That requires empathy, not spreadsheets. Conversation, not conjecture.

Tactical Tip: Conduct 20 interviews before you build anything. Listen more than you speak. Pattern recognition will emerge.

2.2. Competitors: Know Who You're Fighting

Never say "we have no competitors." If there's a problem worth solving, people are already solving it—badly, manually, or with substitutes.

Use the **Competitor Intelligence Map**:

- **Direct**: Who offers similar solutions to the same customer?

- **Indirect**: Who solves the problem differently?

- **Replacement**: What workarounds are people using?

Track:

- Pricing strategies

- Positioning and messaging

- Feature sets and gaps

- Funding and hiring moves

> *"If you know the enemy... you need not fear the result of a hundred battles."*

Understanding their strengths helps you avoid head-on clashes. Spot their weaknesses to identify where you can win. Sometimes, it's in speed. Other times, in UX. Sometimes, just in voice and trust.

2.3. Market Forces: Terrain Intelligence

Sun Tzu devoted an entire section to terrain types. Business terrain changes just as often:

- **Regulatory terrain**: What laws and risks shape your space?

- **Economic terrain**: Are interest rates, consumer spending, or capital flows shifting?

- **Platform terrain**: Are you building on top of a stable foundation (e.g., app stores, APIs) or quicksand?

> *"Those who do not know the conditions of mountains and forests, hazardous defiles, marshes and swamps, cannot conduct the march of an army."*

Today's equivalent? Founders who don't understand market dynamics can't navigate scale or sustainability.

---

3. Internal Alignment: Organize Before You Mobilize

> *"The general who wins a battle makes many calculations in his temple before the battle is fought."*

The temple for entrepreneurs is internal alignment. Your team must know what they are building, why they are building it, and what hill they are climbing together. Alignment is force-multiplying.

3.1. Mission, Vision, and Values

- **Mission**: What change are we driving?

- **Vision**: What does the world look like when we succeed?

- **Values**: How do we behave under pressure?

> *"He will win who has military capacity and is not interfered with by the sovereign."*

In business: The "sovereign" is internal misalignment, unclear goals, or cultural dysfunction. If your team doesn't know the mission, your startup becomes reactive—busy, not effective.

3.2. People: Roles, Not Just Titles

Every player on your team must know:

- What they own

- How success is measured

- How their work ladders up to strategy

Sun Tzu prized discipline, structure, and reward systems.

> *"When rewards are beyond reach, the troops lose interest; when punishments are too severe, they become disheartened."*

Startups require intrinsic motivation and clear systems of recognition. Equity helps—but clarity helps more.

3.3. Communication: Brief Like a Commander

A startup can go to war every week. Standups, sprint reviews, all-hands—each is a briefing. Great generals don't overtalk. They issue clear, motivating commands. Founders should too.

- Keep updates concise.

- Set direction, not just tasks.

- Surface blockers like landmines.

4. Tools: Founder's SWOT and Competitor Intelligence Map

 Strategic introspection and reconnaissance shouldn't stay in your head. They need to be written down, analyzed, and revisited regularly.

4.1. Founder's SWOT Template

Use this template to capture your personal strengths, weaknesses, opportunities, and threats. Revisit it quarterly to track patterns and guide your decisions.

Strengths

- Ask yourself: What do I do better than 90% of people I know?

- Reflect on activities that energize and motivate you.

Weaknesses

- Identify tasks you habitually avoid or consistently underperform.

- Note situations where you overreact or let emotions override judgment.

Opportunities

- List emerging trends, networks, or skill gaps in the market you can uniquely exploit.

- Consider partnerships, certifications, or technology shifts that align with your expertise.

Threats

- Acknowledge personal habits or blind spots that could undermine your venture.

- Challenge your assumptions: which beliefs about your market or yourself might be wrong?

Pro Tip: Fill this out every quarter. Then look back at the past three months' decisions and outcomes. You'll begin to see recurring themes and areas for focused growth.

4.2. Competitor Intelligence Map

Create an evolving dossier on each major rival. Update it live—competitors change fast, and blind spots can cost you market share.

Competitor Name

- **Key Strengths:** What advantages do they hold? (e.g., established brand, network effects)

- **Primary Weaknesses:** Where are they slow or vulnerable? (e.g., outdated UX, limited support)

- **Positioning Statement:** How do they describe themselves in the market? (e.g., "The enterprise choice," "Built for founders")

- **Pricing Tier:** Note their price range or relative positioning ($, $$, $$$).

- **Feature Gaps:** Which capabilities do they lack that you can exploit? (e.g., no mobile integration, missing API)

Action Step: Keep this map in a living document. Review it monthly—and after any competitor announcement or product launch—so you never underestimate how quickly they can pivot.

Conclusion: Preparation Is Power

"Victorious warriors win first and then go to war."

This chapter is your training ground. Success doesn't begin with products or campaigns—it begins with clarity: of self, of market, of mission.

Founders who take the time to truly **know themselves** avoid self-sabotage. Founders who rigorously **study their market** avoid ambushes. And founders who **align their teams** move with power.

In Sun Tzu's world, the war was physical. In yours, it's cognitive. It's informational. It's emotional. But the rules haven't changed.

Know yourself. Know your market. Then move.

Chapter 2: Strategic Positioning Beats Brute Force

"The victorious strategist only seeks battle after the victory has been won." – Sun Tzu

---

Introduction

Too many startups rush to launch, assuming speed alone will guarantee market share. But as Sun Tzu teaches, **victory begins long before the first move**. Strategic positioning—choosing the right problem, the right market, and the right moment—beats brute force every time. This chapter shows how founders can secure wins by planning battles they're already poised to win.

The Danger of Rushing to Launch

Speed kills—especially when it's not paired with clarity. Founders are often told to "move fast and break things," but breaking things without a plan leads to chaos. Sun Tzu warns:

"He will win who knows when to fight and when not to fight."

In the startup world, many lose not because their idea was bad, but because they launched without understanding the terrain.

Premature launches can burn through goodwill, capital, and morale. A half-baked product may hit the market only to be ignored or ridiculed. Press coverage might spike, but what follows is silence. **A poorly positioned launch teaches the market to ignore you.** Recovering from that is harder than waiting.

> *"To be prepared beforehand for any contingency is the greatest of virtues."*

Preparation doesn't mean procrastination—it means deliberate positioning. Know who you're serving, what problem you're solving, and why now is the moment to act.

Case in point: Google didn't rush to compete with Facebook. They tried Google+, failed, and ultimately focused on where they had the edge: search and ads. Meanwhile, competitors who rushed in to mimic Facebook burned trust and money.

Lesson for founders: Don't launch just because you're scared of missing out. **Launch when you've shaped the battlefield to favor your strengths.**

Picking the Right Market Niche Before Scaling

Choosing a market niche is not a compromise—it's a **tactical opening**.

"If he sends reinforcements everywhere, he will everywhere be weak."

Startups that try to serve "everyone" serve no one deeply. Generalized products dilute value. Specificity creates strength.

Early adopters don't want bland tools. They want sharp weapons tailored to their needs. Winning a niche means earning loyalty, feedback, and viral growth. **Focus creates clarity**—in product design, messaging, and execution.

"You can be sure of succeeding in your attacks if you only attack places which are undefended."

Great niches are not guesses. They are **discovered through pain**—pain customers are already feeling, with workarounds they already hate.

Airbnb didn't launch as a hospitality giant. It started with three air mattresses during a conference where hotels were booked solid. The niche was tight, urgent, and underserved.

The ideal niche is:

- Specific enough to own

- Painful enough to demand a solution

- Small enough to move quickly

- Big enough to expand from

Don't try to be a platform before being a product. **Win a single hill before marching on the empire.**

Timing Your Moves: First-Mover vs. Fast-Follower

There's a myth that being first guarantees success. **It doesn't.**

> *"The clever combatant imposes his will on the enemy but does not allow the enemy's will to be imposed on him."*

First-movers pay the tax of education and infrastructure. Fast-followers reverse-engineer the wins and sidestep the losses.

Facebook wasn't the first social network.
Google wasn't the first search engine.
Apple didn't invent the smartphone.

Timing is about leverage, not ego. Sometimes being early just means **being wrong**.

> *"Do not repeat the tactics which have gained you one victory, but let your methods be regulated by the infinite variety of circumstances."*

Use this to evaluate timing:

- **First-mover advantage**: Strong if you have network effects, defensibility, or switching costs.

- **Fast-follower advantage**: Strong if you can move faster, iterate smarter, and market better.

Questions to ask:

- Is the infrastructure mature?

- Is the user behavior established?

- Can we deliver better before they notice?

It's better to be **second with dominance** than first with exhaustion.

Action: Strategic Positioning Canvas

All strategy must translate into action. Here's your tool: the **Strategic Positioning Canvas**. Fill this out **before** you build, fundraise, or launch.

1. Customer Clarity

- Who is your specific, urgent user?

- What problem do they face right now?

- How are they solving it today?

---

2. Competitive Awareness

- Who else is targeting this user?

- Where are they strong?

- Where are they weak?

"If you know the enemy and know yourself, you need not fear the result of a hundred battles."

---

3. Unique Advantage

- What can you do that they can't?

- What do you know that they ignore?

- What gives you structural advantage (data, tech, insight)?

---

4. Timing Insight

- Why is now the right time?

- What changed in the world (tech, law, habits, tools)?

- What's urgent now that wasn't before?

---

5. Expansion Path

- After this niche, what's next?

- Can this wedge expand into a platform or network?

> *"Plan for what is difficult while it is easy, do what is great while it is small."*

Use this canvas with your team. Revisit it often. It prevents panic decisions and anchors you to leverage.

Case Studies & Real-World Parallels

Slack

Origin: Internal tool for a failed game.
They launched slowly, focusing on engineers and small teams.
Their positioning? "Kill email at work."
Result: Product-market fit before mass marketing.

Dropbox

They didn't build a full product first. Instead, they made a video.
This validated interest, drew beta users, and proved demand—before writing code.
Result: Smart positioning saved months of build time.

Zoom

Entered a crowded space. Outperformed by focusing on quality, simplicity, and business use.
Didn't try to be social or trendy—just fast, reliable, and intuitive.
Result: Dominated during COVID while others scrambled.

Quibi

Raised $1.75 billion. Rushed to launch. Ignored signals about user habits and behavior.
Result: Collapsed in under a year.
Why? No strategic positioning. No unique angle. Just brute force.

These case studies show that strategy trumps resources.
Position smart, and you don't need to outspend.

Conclusion: Strategy Is the Real Speed

"To win without fighting is best." – Sun Tzu

Real speed is not motion—it's **momentum**. And momentum comes from **positioning**, not panic.

Strategy means:

- Picking the fight you're set up to win.

- Avoiding the fights that drain you.

- Positioning where you are naturally strong.

"He who is prudent and lies in wait for an enemy who is not, will be victorious."

In business terms: You win when you **prepare better** than others.

Before you build, ask:

- Do we have clarity?

- Are we deploying our strengths?

- Are we playing our own game—or someone else's?

Because in the end, the startups that survive aren't the fastest. They're the ones who **moved with purpose**—and positioned to win.

Chapter 3: The Terrain of Business

"He who knows the terrain gains the upper hand." —
Sun Tzu

Introduction: Strategy Starts with the Ground Beneath You

In war, terrain shapes every decision. A skilled general studies the land before committing troops. In business, the equivalent is your **industry landscape**—the trends, power players, forces, rules, and terrain types that shape your odds of success.

> *"Know the ground, know the weather; your victory will then be total."*

Entrepreneurs often fail not because of bad ideas, but because they operate on bad terrain. They enter markets already captured by giants. They build on fragile ecosystems. They ignore regulatory cliffs.

This chapter arms you with the tools to analyze business terrain as methodically as a commander planning a campaign. We'll break it into four parts:

1. Understanding the industry landscape

2. Knowing the types of terrain

3. Navigating forces like regulation, platforms, and
    ecosystems

4. Mapping opportunity with two practical tools

---

1. Understanding Your Industry Landscape: Trends, Forces, and Players

"If you know the enemy and the terrain, you will not be imperiled in a hundred battles."

Before you act, observe. Your industry isn't just a place—it's a living battlefield full of **shifting patterns**, **power structures**, and **invisible rules**.

1.1 Trends: Signals of Movement

Trends are early signs of where energy and capital are moving. They hint at where the battle might shift.

Ask:

- What behaviors are gaining momentum?

- What technologies are becoming viable?

- What problems are becoming too loud to ignore?

Tactical approach:

- Scan newsletters, investor memos, and hiring trends.

- Watch what big companies are acquiring.

- Observe what startups are pivoting toward.

"Begin by seizing something which your opponent holds dear; then he will be amenable to your will."

Trends often reveal what incumbents value—and fear. If you see a trend they resist, it may be your entry point.

1.2 Forces: What Shapes the Field?

Every market has underlying **forces**. These are not visible at first glance. But they determine your strategic constraints.

The five classic forces (from Porter) still matter:

- **Competitive rivalry**

- **Threat of new entrants**

- **Bargaining power of customers**

- **Bargaining power of suppliers**

- **Threat of substitutes**

But Sun Tzu would also recognize less obvious forces:

- **Distribution power**: Who owns the channels?

- **Cultural shift**: What do people no longer tolerate?

- **Attention dynamics**: What's being ignored?

"Opportunities multiply as they are seized."

Once you see the real forces in play, you stop acting randomly. You start acting surgically.

1.3 Players: Who's Already Fighting?

Map the players in your space. Not just competitors—**everyone with influence**.

Your player map should include:

- Direct competitors (same customer, same solution)

- Indirect competitors (same customer, different solution)

- Substitutes (DIY, status quo, internal teams)

- Platform players (those who control the rails)

- Gatekeepers (institutions, regulators, media, marketplaces)

> *"Do not interfere with an army that is returning home."*

Sometimes you don't attack a giant head-on. You find a flank they're retreating from—or a space they ignore.

Strategy Tip: Look for gaps where the incumbent is overextended, uninterested, or asleep.

---

2. Types of Terrain: Saturated, Fragmented, Emerging

> *"There are five dangerous faults which may affect a general: recklessness, cowardice, a hasty temper, a delicacy of honor, and over-solicitude for his men."*

Startups fail because they misread the **type of terrain** they are operating on. In *The Art of War*, Sun Tzu names many kinds: open ground, difficult terrain, deadly terrain. Here, we map that into business reality.

2.1 Saturated Terrain

Think of a **saturated terrain** as a city with skyscrapers. All the
land is taken. Everyone is shouting. Margins are thin. The winners
already have momentum.

Examples: CRM software, payment processing, eCommerce
platforms.

Challenges:

- Customer acquisition is expensive

- Incumbents have deep moats

- Price wars and feature fatigue

Strategy here:

- Don't try to out-feature giants. Instead, find overlooked
  personas, new messaging angles, or novel distribution
  channels.

- Specialize until you're unignorable.

> *"Attack him where he is unprepared, appear where
> you are not expected."*

Slack didn't win by being better at chat. It won by reframing it:
team collaboration, not messaging. It found space in a saturated
field by changing the frame.

2.2 Fragmented Terrain

Fragmented terrain is scattered. No clear leader. Many small players. Customers are frustrated, switching tools often.

Examples: construction tech, local services, legacy B2B verticals.

Opportunities:

- Consolidate value across tools

- Build a brand people trust

- Offer end-to-end solutions

Caution:

- Fragmented terrain often hides deep complexity. Each niche may have unique workflows or regulations.

> *"When the enemy is relaxed, make them toil. When full, starve them. When settled, make them move."*

In fragmented markets, movement is your edge. Be the first to offer simplicity.

2.3 Emerging Terrain

This is where legends are made. New spaces. No rules. No incumbents. High risk, high return.

Examples: AI-native tools, decentralized governance, synthetic biology, climate tech.

Advantages:

- You can shape user expectations

- You can define the category

- You can move fast without blockers

Risks:

- Customer behaviors are not established

- Infrastructure may be immature

- Timing may be too early

> *"He who is destined to defeat first fights and afterwards looks for victory."*

In emerging markets, **you're building the map while exploring it**. Make sure you're not just inventing—**you're solving**.

---

3. Navigating Regulation, Platforms, and Ecosystems

"The general who advances without coveting fame and retreats without fearing disgrace, whose only thought is to protect his country and do good service for his sovereign, is the jewel of the kingdom."

In business, **sovereigns are platforms, regulators, and ecosystems.** They can bless you—or bury you.

3.1 Regulation: The Hidden Battlefield

Regulation can be wall, weapon, or windfall.

Understand:

- What regulations shape your market?

- Are there compliance advantages you can build into your product?

- Is the law changing in your favor or against you?

"In difficult ground, keep steadily on the march."

If you're in a highly regulated industry (health, fintech, energy), your product must be born with legal strategy built in. Don't tack it on later.

Pro move: Use compliance as a moat. Build trust. Be the first to comply, then use that position to win market share.

3.2 Platforms: Playing on Borrowed Land

If your product relies on Apple, Google, Facebook, Amazon, Salesforce, or any other big platform—you're not building on land. You're camping.

Platforms can:

- Change policies

- Cut off APIs

- Launch copycat products

> *"If you lay siege to a walled city, you must be prepared for a long time."*

Don't bet everything on a platform unless you're also building escape routes. **Own the relationship with your customer**, even if the transaction happens elsewhere.

Platform strategy tips:

- Diversify integrations

- Build your own channels

- Stay close to platform policy changes

3.3 Ecosystems: Allies, Enemies, and Interdependence

Some markets operate like ecosystems. No single player dominates, but many depend on each other. Think logistics, fintech, developer tools.

> *"The highest form of generalship is to balk the enemy's plans."*

You don't have to crush your competition—you can **out-partner them**. Identify who wins when you win. Build alliances. Interoperate. Form co-selling channels.

In ecosystems, winning alone is rare. Winning together is strategy.

---

4. Action Tools: Industry Terrain Map + Opportunity Matrix

Sun Tzu's brilliance came not from theory, but from execution. Let's translate this into two tactical tools.

4.1 Industry Terrain Map

This map helps you classify your current battleground.

Step 1: Classify Your Market Terrain

- Saturated

- Fragmented

- Emerging

Step 2: Identify the Forces in Play

- Regulation

- Platform dependency

- Pricing pressure

- Behavior inertia

Step 3: Locate the Power Players

List key incumbents, platforms, gatekeepers. What's their grip? What are their blind spots?

Step 4: Position Your Company

- What space do you control?

- What space can you flank?

- Where can you build leverage?

4.2. Opportunity Matrix

To decide where to focus your efforts, assess each potential opportunity along two dimensions: **Strategic Fit** (how closely it aligns with your core strengths, mission, and long-term goals, on a scale of 1–5) and **Terrain Advantage** (how favorable the competitive landscape is—weak incumbents, high customer pain, on a scale of 1–5).

- **Niche #1**

    - **Strategic Fit:** 4

    - **Terrain Advantage:** 3

    - **Notes:** Mid-market SaaS space with moderate competition. You have relevant experience, but you'll need to differentiate on user experience and service.

- **Niche #2**

    - **Strategic Fit:** 5

    - **Terrain Advantage:** 5

    - **Notes:** A high-pain problem area where existing players are weak. Your team's expertise lines up perfectly with customer needs and the market is ripe for disruption.

- **Niche #3**

    - **Strategic Fit:** 2

    - **Terrain Advantage:** 4

    - **Notes:** Trending technology with enthusiastic early adopters, but it doesn't play to your current capabilities or brand.

Once you've scored each opportunity, plot them mentally (or on a simple two-axis sketch) and zero in on the ones that score high on both Strategic Fit and Terrain Advantage. These "high-fit, high-advantage" areas represent your best chance at "victory before the battle" — moves where you can quickly establish leadership with the least resistance.

Conclusion: Win the Ground Before the War

"He who knows the terrain gains the upper hand."

Great founders are not just product builders. They are terrain readers. They observe the landscape, find the open paths, and position their company where the odds of winning are stacked in their favor.

Before you build, **map the market**.
Before you scale, **classify the terrain**.
Before you invest, **understand the forces**.

Brute force is expensive. Position is priceless.

So ask yourself:

- Do I truly know my terrain?

- Am I playing to my advantage?

- Are we moving forward—or just moving?

In business, as in war, **where you fight is half the battle.**

Chapter 4: Attack Where the Enemy Is Unprepared

"Attack him where he is unprepared, appear where you are not expected." – Sun Tzu

---

Introduction: Surprise Wins Wars and Markets

Success in entrepreneurship isn't always about building the best product. It's often about **striking where others are vulnerable**—not where they are strong. Sun Tzu's strategy wasn't domination by force. It was about **disruption through insight, timing, and cunning**.

Modern startups don't beat giants with size. They win by finding weaknesses, choosing unexpected angles, and striking fast while incumbents move slow.

This chapter will teach you to:

- Pinpoint the soft spots in your competitors

- Find non-obvious ways to stand out

- Move with precision and speed

- Use a Competitor Weakness Identification Worksheet to guide action

---

1. Finding Weak Spots in the Competition

"If your opponent is of choleric temper, seek to irritate him. Pretend to be weak, that he may grow arrogant."

Sun Tzu understood a fundamental truth: your enemy's strength often hides a weakness. In business, that means the market leaders aren't invincible. In fact, they often carry blind spots—baked into their success.

Your job is to **observe where they fail to serve the customer**, not where they dominate.

1.1 Look for Frustrated Customers

All it takes is one underserved group to open a wedge. Even dominant products can leave users unsatisfied.

Examples:

- Salesforce is powerful but overwhelming—leaves room for simpler CRM tools like Close or Pipedrive.

- Adobe Creative Suite is robust—but bloated—leaves space for Figma or Canva.

- Uber built convenience—but eroded driver trust—opened space for driver-owned platforms.

"When you surround an army, leave an outlet. Do not press a desperate foe too hard."

In business, this means don't just destroy—**liberate**. Offer users what the incumbent won't.

1.2 Find Technical or Structural Inflexibility

Big companies move slow for a reason. They are optimized for **scale, not speed.** Their systems, policies, and org charts are often outdated.

Signs of rigidity:

- They ignore customer feedback loops.

- They can't ship fast or pivot quickly.

- They resist transparency or cultural trends.

"There are roads which must not be followed, armies which must not be attacked."

Don't chase giants head-on. Exploit their inertia. If they've painted themselves into a corner with legacy systems or politics, that's your opening.

1.3 Examine Their Business Model Weaknesses

Every business model has a tradeoff.

Examples:

- If the competitor relies on ad revenue, are they compromising user experience?

- If they serve enterprises, are they ignoring SMBs?

- If they scale with low-touch, are they failing in customer success?

When you understand where they make their money, you understand **where they're unwilling to change**.

> "If he is secure at all points, be prepared for him. If he is in superior strength, evade him."

You don't need to win everywhere. You just need to win **somewhere they can't afford to compete**.

---

2. Zig When Others Zag: Unconventional Positioning

"In the midst of chaos, there is also opportunity."

When every company in your space copies each other's language, UX, and positioning—you have a massive opportunity to **stand out simply by being different**.

Positioning is how you frame your value. It's what people remember about you. When others zag, zig.

2.1 Use Voice and Tone as a Weapon

Most companies sound the same. Safe. Corporate. Predictable.

Opportunity: Be bold, casual, honest, or funny. Sound like a real human, not a legal department.

Example:

- Mailchimp used quirky illustrations and witty microcopy to stand out in a world of bland enterprise email tools.

- Slack's onboarding and loading messages made the tool feel personal—while competitors felt robotic.

"Rouse him, and learn the principle of his activity or inactivity."

In modern marketing: disrupt attention. Make people feel something. That alone creates strategic leverage.

2.2 Reframe the Product Category

You don't always need to invent a new product—just frame the existing one **in a new way**.

Examples:

- Peloton didn't sell exercise bikes. They sold a connected fitness **community**.

- Notion didn't say "we're another document editor." They said: "Your all-in-one workspace."

- Loom didn't compete with Zoom. They pitched asynchronous video—**a new category.**

> *"Appear at points which the enemy must hasten to defend."*

Make the incumbent play **your** game—not theirs. That's the power of framing.

2.3 Choose an Unexpected Audience

Serve customers others overlook.

Examples:

- Zoom targeted remote business teams before everyone else cared.

- Shopify focused on small online sellers, while Amazon chased the enterprise and owned inventory.

- Duolingo targeted casual language learners with gamification, while Rosetta Stone chased formality.

"He who knows when he can fight and when he cannot, will be victorious."

You don't need every customer. You need **the right ignored customer**.

---

3. Outmaneuvering Big Players with Speed and Surprise

"Speed is the essence of war. Take advantage of the enemy's unreadiness."

Startups win not by matching force, but by using **speed, surprise, and focus**.

Big companies are stuck in meetings. You can move. Now.

3.1 Move Faster Than They Can React

Use your size as an advantage. In a startup, decisions can be made in a day. Products can ship in weeks. Marketing campaigns can pivot in hours.

Tactics:

- Build in public—share your roadmap and progress to attract fans and users.

- Launch small, test fast, iterate daily.

- Use direct channels (social, newsletters, DMs) instead of paid ads only.

> *"To rely on rustics and not prepare is the greatest of crimes; to be prepared beforehand for any contingency is the greatest of virtues."*

Be prepared, but act fast. Study. Then strike.

3.2 Create Strategic Surprise

Surprise isn't chaos—it's **calculated unpredictability**.

You can surprise competitors by:

- Launching in a vertical they assumed was dead

- Offering a pricing model they didn't think was viable (e.g., freemium)

- Serving customers they neglected

> *"When you are near, make it appear that you are far away; when far away, that you are near."*

Keep your moves quiet until you're ready to make noise. Then go big. Make the market scramble to catch up.

3.3 Use Focus as a Weapon

Big companies are diluted. You are not. Focused execution creates momentum. Momentum creates wins.

Examples:

- Basecamp stayed tiny and profitable while everyone chased unicorn status.

- Superhuman stayed in private beta until they were truly exceptional.

- Calendly picked one thing (meeting scheduling) and nailed it.

> *"If the enemy is taking his ease, harass him; if well supplied, cut off his supplies."*

While giants optimize for stability, you optimize for **shockwaves**.

4. Action: Competitor Weakness Identification Worksheet

Sun Tzu believed in careful preparation and battlefield intelligence. Here's how to do it for your startup.

Use this **Competitor Weakness Identification Worksheet** with your team.

Step 1: List Top Competitors

Include both direct rivals and indirect alternatives to paint a full competitive picture.

Competitor A

- **Product Strengths:** Offers an exceptionally robust feature set that addresses most enterprise requirements out of the box.

- **Market Strengths:** Commands strong brand trust and recognition, benefiting from long-standing customer relationships and extensive marketing reach.

- **Blind Spots:** Their user experience is often criticized as overly complex, and customers report slow response times from support teams.

- **Risk Areas:** Heavy regulatory scrutiny around their data practices and compliance creates potential liabilities you can exploit.

Competitor B

- **Product Strengths:** Boasts a clean, simple user interface that customers adopt quickly with minimal training.

- **Market Strengths:** Competes aggressively on price, undercutting larger players to attract cost-sensitive buyers.

- **Blind Spots:** Integration capabilities are limited, forcing customers to build workarounds or use third-party connectors.

- **Risk Areas:** Their focus on a narrow segment makes them vulnerable to shifts in that niche and exposes them to market concentration risk.

Step 2: Find Common Pain Points

Ask real customers:

- What do you hate about [competitor]?

- What features do you never use?

- What do they do badly that we can do better?

Step 3: Identify Inflexibility

For each competitor:

- What would be hard for them to change?

- What markets or features are they avoiding?

- What constraints do their shareholders or legacy code create?

Step 4: Craft a Flank Attack Plan

Based on your findings:

- Who can you serve better?

- What feature can you own?

- What messaging can you dominate?

"In war, let your great object be victory, not lengthy campaigns."

Pick one weakness. Exploit it fully. Don't try to win everywhere.

Conclusion: Precision Beats Power

"Victorious warriors win first and then go to war, while defeated warriors go to war first and then seek to win."

Founders who succeed don't just build. They outthink, outmaneuver, and outposition their competition.

Don't fight the battle they expect. **Fight the one they forgot.**

- Find the cracks in their armor.

- Be where they're not.

- Speak what they won't.

- Move while they wait.

Attack where the enemy is unprepared. Appear where you are not expected.

That's how you turn a small startup into a serious threat—and a serious threat into a market winner.

Chapter 5: Build an Army That Wins Without Fighting

"The supreme art of war is to subdue the enemy without fighting." – Sun Tzu

---

Introduction: Victory Without Violence

In *The Art of War*, Sun Tzu elevates the concept of winning without fighting to the highest form of strategic mastery. Applied to entrepreneurship, this means building a business that **wins without friction**, attracts customers organically, and disarms competition before the battle even begins.

True product and brand strength isn't about domination. It's about **pulling people toward you**, not pushing against them. It's about **creating gravity** so strong that users, talent, and partners want to orbit you.

This chapter covers:

- Building a product so good it sells itself

- Crafting a brand and narrative people want to follow

- Building alliances that expand your reach and resilience

- An actionable framework: The Product-Led Growth
  Strategy Planner

---

1. Building a Product So Good It Markets Itself

"In the midst of chaos, there is also opportunity."

The first and most powerful path to victory is creating a product so valuable, so elegant, so essential that customers become your salesforce.

This is the engine of **Product-Led Growth (PLG)**: when the product itself drives acquisition, retention, and expansion—without relying on salespeople or ads.

1.1 Start With Obsessive Product Quality

A great product solves a real problem better than anything else. But that's not enough. It has to do it **clearly**, **quickly**, and **consistently**.

"Opportunities multiply as they are seized."

Every moment your user interacts with your product is a chance to impress—or to lose them. Delight becomes a weapon. So does reliability. So does clarity.

Examples:

- Calendly eliminated the back-and-forth of scheduling with one link. It didn't just solve a problem—it erased it.

- Notion turned complexity into clarity with modular tools and beautiful UX.

- Superhuman made email feel powerful again, not painful.

Tactical edge: Reduce user time-to-value. Get them to the "aha" moment **fast**.

1.2 Remove Friction Relentlessly

Every point of confusion is a crack in your momentum. Every unpolished detail invites churn.

> *"When the strike of a hawk breaks the body of its prey, it is because of timing."*

Your onboarding, UI, and performance must strike like a hawk—fast, clean, lethal. Users don't give second chances.

Focus on:

- Seamless onboarding

- Lightning-fast load times

- Simple and intuitive navigation

- In-app education, not PDFs or YouTube searches

Let your product *explain itself*.

1.3 Make Sharing Inevitable

A self-marketing product embeds its own virality. It makes sharing **natural**, not forced.

Examples:

- Dropbox gave free storage for referrals.

- Loom made sharing video as easy as sending a link.

- Figma allowed live collaboration—pulling entire teams in.

> *"He will win who prepares himself and waits to take the enemy unprepared."*

While others cold email or blast ads, your users invite others to join. No ads. No begging. Just **natural spread**.

---

2. Leveraging Brand, Narrative, and Loyalty

> *"Victorious warriors win first and then go to war."*

Founders often obsess over product and neglect brand. This is a mistake. **Brand is the emotional moat**. It turns customers into advocates and employees into believers.

2.1 Define the Narrative

Your narrative is not your slogan. It's your **why**, your **mission**, and your **enemy**. People follow stories, not specs.

Examples:

- Tesla isn't "just electric cars." It's acceleration toward a clean energy future.

- Patagonia isn't "just outdoor gear." It's rebellion against disposable culture.

- Stripe isn't "just payments." It's the economic infrastructure of the internet.

"All warfare is based on deception."

A compelling story shapes perception. You control what the market sees and believes. Even if your features are similar, your story can be radically different.

2.2 Be Unmistakable in Brand

Your brand should have a distinct personality—visible in every touchpoint.

Ask:

- Would someone recognize our website in 3 seconds?

- Is our tone consistent in tweets, emails, error messages?

- Do we feel alive—or like a template?

Example: Mailchimp's quirky tone made them loveable. Even their 404 pages were in character.

> *"When you are strong, appear weak. When you are weak, appear strong."*

Use brand to punch above your weight. A strong voice makes you look bigger, bolder, and more trusted.

2.3 Cultivate True Loyalty

Loyalty isn't built by features. It's built by **connection**, **consistency**, and **care**.

Do you:

- Reward your early adopters?

- Celebrate your users' wins?

- Respond like a human, not a helpdesk?

Real loyalty survives product glitches. It turns into referrals, testimonials, and second chances.

3. Creating Alliances, Partnerships, and Ecosystems

"If you know the enemy and know yourself, you need not fear the result of a hundred battles."

You don't need to fight every battle alone. Strategic alliances can give you access to new markets, credibility, capabilities, and cover.

3.1 Choose Strategic Allies

The best partnerships do one of three things:

- **Extend distribution**: someone sells your product

- **Add credibility**: someone vouches for your legitimacy

- **Add capability**: someone strengthens your offering

Examples:

- Shopify partners with apps to expand its ecosystem.

- Atlassian integrated with Slack to increase usage.

- Apple lets other platforms create accessories—creating gravitational pull.

> *"There are routes not to be followed, armies not to be attacked."*

Don't partner randomly. Partner where **value exchange is natural and complementary**.

3.2 Create Platform Gravity

Instead of building everything, build **platforms** that attract others to build with you.

Why?

- You multiply value without multiplying effort.

- You make switching harder for users.

- You create a self-sustaining flywheel.

> *"Those skilled in war subdue the enemy's forces without going to battle."*

This is exactly what platforms do. They attract, integrate, and **defuse competition** by inviting them in.

Examples:

- Salesforce AppExchange

- Notion API + integrations

- Stripe Connect

3.3 Leverage Communities and Networks

Communities extend your power without expanding your payroll. They make users **feel like owners**.

Tactics:

- Launch ambassador programs

- Host user-led events or webinars

- Highlight customer-created templates, plug-ins, or use cases

> *"Treat your men as you would your own beloved sons.
> And they will follow you into the deepest valley."*

That's how you treat your users. And in return, they become your army.

4. Action: Product-Led Growth Strategy Planner

This tool will help you implement everything above. Fill it out with your team, revisit quarterly.

Step 1: Define Core Product Value

- What's the #1 problem your product solves?

- How quickly can a new user experience that value?

Step 2: Identify Friction Points

- Where do users drop off during onboarding?

- What steps confuse or frustrate them?

- What features go unused—and why?

Step 3: Build Virality Loops

- How does one user invite or involve others?

- What incentive exists for them to share or refer?

- How is content or value created that draws others in?

Step 4: Clarify Your Narrative

- What story are you telling?

- Who is the hero? (Hint: It's the user, not you.)

- What enemy are you helping them defeat?

Step 5: Craft Brand Consistency

- Is your voice the same across channels?

- Do you sound distinct from competitors?

- Would your website, app, or tweet be unmistakably yours?

Step 6: Map Alliance Opportunities

- Who already has your customers?

- Who could benefit from your success?

- What integrations would unlock new channels?

Step 7: Design Community Flywheels

- How do you make users feel seen and valued?

- Where can they connect with each other?

- What recognition, tools, or roles can you give them?

"He wins his battles by making no mistakes."

This planner is your tool to avoid mistakes—and build a product and movement so good, you win without a fight.

Conclusion: Subdue Without a Fight

"To capture the enemy's entire army is better than to destroy it."

Entrepreneurship doesn't require a battlefield full of broken competitors. It requires **clarity**, **craft**, and **connection**.

You don't need to shout. Let your product speak.
 You don't need to chase. Let your story pull.
 You don't need to crush. Let your allies lift.

The best companies win not with weapons, but with **magnetism**.

They build armies of users, fans, and partners who don't just buy—but believe.

That's what it means to **subdue the enemy without fighting**.

Chapter 6: Speed is a Weapon

"Speed is the essence of war. Take advantage of the enemy's unreadiness." – Sun Tzu

---

Introduction: Speed as Strategy

In the modern startup battlefield, the ability to **move quickly and decisively** is one of your greatest weapons. You're not competing against just better-funded players—you're competing against time, indecision, bureaucracy, and stagnation.

Sun Tzu understood that in war, speed wasn't just about movement—it was about **momentum, surprise, and adaptability**. It was about acting before your opponent could react. In business, the same holds true: success often belongs to those who **learn and act faster** than anyone else.

This chapter will explore:

- Why decision velocity is a competitive edge

- How lean startup principles create speed

- Why killing ideas is strategic, not wasteful

- A tactical tool: the Speed Execution Dashboard

---

1. Decision Velocity as Competitive Edge

"Speed is the essence of war."

Your startup's ability to make decisions—fast, frequent, and accurate—is a force multiplier. Slowness kills. Especially when you're small, every day of indecision is a day your runway burns and competitors gain ground.

1.1 What Is Decision Velocity?

It's not about reckless speed. It's about how quickly and confidently your team can:

- Recognize new data

- Make a decision

- Act on it

- Learn and adapt

"When the strike of a hawk breaks the body of its prey, it is because of timing."

Timing is everything. Founders who wait for perfect information are always too late. The best decisions are made with 70% certainty—and iterated on the rest.

1.2 Why Startups Must Decide Faster

Large companies can afford to delay. You can't. Your agility **is** your edge. It lets you:

- Seize opportunities your competitors haven't seen

- Respond to market feedback in real time

- Out-execute on strategy even with fewer resources

"The good fighters of old first put themselves beyond the possibility of defeat, and then waited for an opportunity of defeating the enemy."

Speed creates defense (by staying ahead) and offense (by catching others flat-footed).

1.3 How to Build a Culture of Speed

Speed is not just tactics. It's culture. And culture comes from the top.

Ask yourself:

- Do we prioritize clarity over consensus?

- Do we empower people to ship without constant approvals?

- Do we punish mistakes—or reward learning?

Speed doesn't mean chaos. It means **structured boldness**.

---

2. Lean Startup Principles: Test Fast, Learn Fast, Iterate

"If quick, I survive. If not quick, I am lost."

Eric Ries' Lean Startup methodology and Sun Tzu's doctrine share the same soul: **adapt, adjust, accelerate**. Test ideas fast. Learn what works. Discard what doesn't. And do it all before your enemy knows what hit them.

2.1 Build–Measure–Learn Loop

This is the foundation:

1. **Build**: Create the smallest version of your idea.

2. **Measure**: See how users interact with it.

3. **Learn**: Decide what to keep, kill, or double down on.

> *"Do not engage an enemy who has conquered all else. Attack where he is not prepared."*

This is what MVPs are for—not to launch weak products, but to test in stealth, before the competition notices.

2.2 Minimum Viable ≠ Minimum Effort

Too many confuse MVP with sloppy. An MVP should:

- Deliver core value

- Be easy to use

- Prove a hypothesis

Example:
 Dropbox didn't build a full file-sharing platform. They made a video demo. That demo proved demand—before writing a line of code.

> *"Appear at points which the enemy must hasten to defend; march swiftly to places where you are not expected."*

Your MVP is a sneak attack. A test. A probe into enemy territory to measure their defenses.

2.3 Run Multiple Experiments in Parallel

Never bet the house on one idea. Bet small. Bet often. Run multiple experiments. Let data, not ego, decide.

Examples:

- A/B test landing pages with different positioning.

- Run 3–4 acquisition channels simultaneously in small bursts.

- Launch internal tools or scripts to automate repetitive tasks and study the results.

> *"In war, numbers alone confer no advantage."*

Speed, direction, and flexibility beat brute force every time.

---

3. Killing Ideas Quickly and Moving On

> *"He will win who knows how to handle both superior and inferior forces."*

One of the most dangerous things in a startup is a **zombie idea**—an initiative that's not dead but not alive. It's burning time and money but not delivering value.

Learning to **kill fast** is one of the highest forms of startup discipline.

3.1 Why Founders Struggle to Kill Ideas

- Emotional attachment ("This was my vision.")

- Sunk cost fallacy ("We've already invested six months.")

- Team pressure ("We hired a whole team to build this.")

- Public perception ("We can't backtrack now.")

But remember:

> *"To subdue the enemy without fighting is the acme of skill."*

That includes subduing **your own ego**. You are not your idea. Killing it is not failure. It's evolution.

3.2 Signs It's Time to Kill

- Users don't care, no matter how much you market

- The core metric isn't improving after multiple iterations

- Your team is demoralized or constantly firefighting

Ask: If this weren't already built, would we build it again?

If not—kill it.

> *"Do not pursue an enemy who simulates flight; do not attack soldiers whose temper is keen."*

Don't fall for traps. Sometimes the idea lingers because it feels close to working. That's often a mirage.

3.3 What Happens After You Kill

- Resources are freed

- Morale often improves (clarity is energizing)

- You open space for better bets

Celebrate the kill. Conduct a mini postmortem. Log the lesson. Then move on.

> *"If quick, I survive. If not quick, I am lost."*

It's not the mistake that kills you. It's how long you live with it.

---

4. Action: Speed Execution Dashboard

This dashboard is your operating system for running a high-velocity team. Review it weekly. Use it to guide decisions, surface blockers, and accelerate progress.

Step 1: Track Decision Time

- How long does it take us to make product decisions?

- What's slowing it down (approval layers, lack of data, fear)?

Target: 24–72 hours max for tactical decisions. 1 week max for strategic ones.

Step 2: Monitor Build–Measure–Learn Loops

- What's the average time from idea → MVP → test → iteration?

- Are experiments happening every week?

Target: 2–4 week full cycle per test.

Step 3: Maintain an Idea Graveyard

- What projects have we paused, killed, or deprioritized?

- What did we learn?

Why: You must **honor the kills**. Document them. Study them.
Don't repeat them.

Step 4: Velocity Standups

Daily or weekly, ask:

- What did we ship?

- What did we learn?

- What's stuck?

Keep updates short. Focus on outcomes, not activity.

Step 5: Blocker Escalation Protocol

Every day lost to indecision or confusion is compounding waste.

Ask:

- Where is clarity missing?

- Who needs to decide?

- What's the deadline?

"Speed is the essence of war."

Put this quote at the top of your sprint board.

Conclusion: Speed Is the Great Equalizer

"He who is prudent and lies in wait for an enemy who is not, will be victorious."

Speed isn't chaos. It's control. It's discipline. It's clarity.

Your startup's job is not to be bigger. It's to be **faster to learn**, faster to ship, and faster to adjust.

Move faster than your fear.
 Decide faster than your competitors.
 Kill faster than your ego wants to.

"Opportunities multiply as they are seized."

Speed creates opportunity. Opportunity creates leverage. Leverage creates success.

So build the culture. Build the dashboards. Build the mindset.

And move.

Chapter 7: Deception, Discipline, and Psychological Advantage

"All warfare is based on deception." – Sun Tzu

Introduction: Mind Games and Market Moves

Sun Tzu's treatise is not just a manual for combat. It's a masterclass in psychology. He understood that war is not only fought with weapons but with perception, discipline, and leverage.

Entrepreneurship is no different. In a market filled with noise, the sharpest founders win not only with great products, but with **sharp positioning, relentless consistency, and psychological advantage**.

To build a resilient business, you must play more than just the visible game. You must understand:

- The story your brand tells before anyone tries your product

- The way internal discipline shapes external momentum

- How pricing, negotiation, and message control can shape reality

This chapter breaks down:

- Using brand and perception as weapons

- The power of discipline in day-to-day execution

- Psychological tactics in pricing, positioning, and negotiations

- The Psychological Leverage Toolkit for practical deployment

---

1. Branding and Perception: Creating Asymmetry

"Appear weak when you are strong, and strong when you are weak."

Perception is your most underutilized weapon. In battle, deception is used to confuse, delay, mislead, and provoke. In business, your brand—how you appear to the world—can achieve the same effects.

Great brands win by creating **asymmetry**: they look bigger than they are, move faster than expected, and say what no one else dares to.

1.1 Appear Strong Even When Small

Startups can't outspend, but they can out-position.

Tactics to create asymmetric perception:

- Speak with bold confidence in your messaging

- Use crisp, clean, premium design

- Signal traction with real metrics, even if small ("1,000 companies onboarded in 90 days")

> *"In the midst of chaos, there is also opportunity."*

In crowded spaces, customers crave clarity. If you look composed and confident, they'll follow.

1.2 Be Where They Don't Expect

Big players have predictable channels: PR, trade shows, and legacy platforms. You can strike where they aren't looking.

- Use memes and humor to go viral

- Go grassroots in small communities or subcultures

- Embed in creator ecosystems instead of buying billboard ads

Example: Liquid Death (canned water) grew fast by **acting like a metal band**, not a wellness brand.

> *"Attack him where he is unprepared, appear where you are not expected."*

Your edge is unexpectedness. Weaponize it.

1.3 Craft a Polarizing Narrative

People don't remember brands that play it safe. They remember brands that **stand for something**—even if it alienates some.

Tactics:

- Position against a villain (outdated industry norms, bloated incumbents, broken UX)

- Build a story around rebellion or revolution

- Create content that challenges the status quo

> *"Let your plans be dark and impenetrable as night, and when you move, fall like a thunderbolt."*

When your brand finally gets noticed, let it **drop like lightning**.

---

2. Discipline in Execution: Routines, Rituals, Accountability

"The general who advances without coveting fame and retreats without fearing disgrace, whose only thought is to protect his country, is the jewel of the kingdom."

In startups, most failure is **not strategic—it's operational**. What kills teams isn't lack of ideas; it's lack of discipline.

If perception wins attention, **discipline delivers results.** Speed without structure is chaos. Creativity without accountability is waste.

2.1 Establish Execution Rituals

Your startup needs daily and weekly routines to sustain progress.

Examples:

- Daily standups: focus, unblock, align

- Weekly sprint planning: commit, prioritize, execute

- Monthly strategy reviews: zoom out, adjust, refocus

"Plan for what is difficult while it is easy, do what is great while it is small."

Discipline today prevents disaster tomorrow.

2.2 Create Internal Cadence

Discipline is about rhythm. Set a drumbeat for your company.

- OKRs (Objectives and Key Results) every quarter

- Weekly metrics reviews

- Regular 1:1s to align individuals

Make performance visible, but without blame. **Accountability must be cultural, not punitive.**

> *"When the men are punished before they have grown attached to you, they will not prove submissive."*

Win loyalty first. Then demand excellence.

2.3 Audit Time and Focus Ruthlessly

Where time goes, results follow.

Ask:

- Are we building or just planning?

- Are meetings productive or performative?

- What are we doing that doesn't move metrics?

Knowing yourself includes **knowing where you waste effort.**

---

3. Negotiation Tactics, Pricing Psychology, and Controlling Narratives

"Supreme excellence consists of breaking the enemy's resistance without fighting."

Every part of business involves persuasion. Selling your product, raising money, forming partnerships—it's all negotiation.

And negotiation isn't about shouting louder. It's about **reading the room, shaping the frame, and controlling the pace.**

3.1 Framing is Everything

The way you frame a conversation determines how others see value.

Tactics:

- Anchor high in pricing discussions ("Most customers start at $2,000/month")

- Use scarcity strategically ("We're only accepting 5 new clients this quarter.")

- Reposition objections as opportunities ("That's exactly why people switch to us.")

> *"Build your opponent a golden bridge to retreat across."*

Never trap someone in a negotiation. Give them a way to say yes without losing face.

3.2 Pricing Psychology

Price signals value. Underpricing is as risky as overpricing.

Tactical principles:

- Use charm pricing ($29 → $29.99) to increase conversions

- Offer tiered pricing to guide choices (decoy effect)

- Use "pay what you want" or free trials to reduce barrier and build habit

> *"Ponder and deliberate before you make a move."*

Set pricing as a strategy, not a guess. You're shaping perception—not just cost.

3.3 Control the Narrative

Narrative control isn't just branding. It's how you **shape investor conversations, pitch decks, feature announcements**, and more.

Narrative tactics:

- Define your own metrics (e.g., "time to ROI" instead of "monthly active users")

- Tell your growth story with leading indicators (engagement before revenue)

- Publish thought leadership to frame how people see your category

> *"He who knows how to deceive will always find someone who is willing to be deceived."*

Control doesn't mean manipulation—it means choosing what story people hear first.

---

4. Action: Psychological Leverage Toolkit

This toolkit turns abstract psychology into tactical levers. Use it in team meetings, fundraising, product strategy, and customer engagement.

Toolkit Component 1: Perception Amplifier

- What signals can we use to look bigger (logos, partnerships, metrics)?

- How can we reframe our size as speed or agility?

- What unexpected brand voice or visuals can cut through noise?

Toolkit Component 2: Execution Discipline Audit

- What routines guide our weekly work?

- How do we surface blockers?

- Where is discipline weak (and why)?

Toolkit Component 3: Negotiation Playbook

- What's our pricing floor and ceiling?

- What common objections do we flip?

- How do we introduce scarcity, urgency, or exclusivity?

Toolkit Component 4: Narrative Control Checklist

- Are we setting the frame or reacting to it?

- What language are we using to describe our growth?

- What story are we telling about our mission—and is it landing?

Toolkit Component 5: Internal Ritual Map

- What weekly and monthly rhythms drive accountability?

- What metrics do we track consistently?

- What habits support or sabotage performance?

"The wise warrior avoids the battle."

These tools help you win **before** the battle even begins.

Conclusion: Mind Over Muscle

"To know your enemy, you must become your enemy."

Psychological advantage isn't about manipulation. It's about understanding perception, discipline, and decision-making better than your competitors.

- Use your brand to strike like a mirage: unpredictable, bold, and unforgettable.

- Use rituals to turn chaos into focus and motion into momentum.

- Use pricing and framing not just to sell, but to lead the conversation.

- Use narrative to control what the market sees, hears, and expects.

Sun Tzu didn't teach dominance. He taught **mastery**—of self, of the opponent, of timing and terrain.

Build your startup the same way:
Calm outside. Ruthless inside.
Disciplined. Deceptive. Decisive.

And in every room you enter—customer, investor, competitor—carry this truth:

"All warfare is based on deception."

Now go shape what they see.

Chapter 8: Leadership That Commands Loyalty and Action

"Regard your soldiers as your children, and they will follow you into the deepest valleys." – Sun Tzu

---

Introduction: The General of the Startup Army

In war, the general determines not only the strategy—but the spirit. In startups, the founder or CEO fills this role. You are not just a strategist or executor. You are the **emotional nucleus** of your company. You decide how people act in a crisis, what they believe in the fog, and whether they fight or freeze when things go sideways.

Sun Tzu didn't preach fear-based leadership. He preached a style built on **respect, mission, and clarity**. The kind that doesn't just generate output, but inspires sacrifice.

Startups thrive or die not just because of funding or features—but because of how well the people inside them are led.

This chapter focuses on:

- How to build a culture of trust, grit, and clarity

- How to lead through uncertainty and chaos

- How to align incentives and rally your team around a
  mission

- An actionable framework: The Culture Codex + Leadership
  Audit

---

1. Building a Culture of Trust, Grit, and Clarity

> *"When you lay down a rule, begin by enforcing it with
> iron discipline; then when your soldiers have grown
> used to it, you can relax the severity."*

Culture is the operating system of your company. It defines how
people behave when no one is watching. It governs whether your
team withers under pressure or rises to meet it.

1.1 Trust: The Foundation of Execution

Trust doesn't mean agreeing all the time. It means believing in
each other's intent, integrity, and follow-through.

Trust-building behaviors:

- Radical transparency about goals, metrics, and risks

- Sharing decision-making context—not just orders

- Admitting mistakes at the top to model accountability

> *"If his forces are united, separate them. If sovereign and subject are in accord, put between them some distance."*

This is how competitors try to break you—from the inside. Unity is your defense.

1.2 Grit: Building a Team That Doesn't Flinch

Startups are hard. Your team will face failed launches, fundraising stress, customer churn, and personal burnout. Your job is to **build muscle**, not just morale.

How to build grit:

- Normalize challenges—don't hide or sugarcoat them

- Celebrate effort, not just outcome

- Talk about previous company battles—and how they were overcome

> *"The skillful fighter puts himself into a position which makes defeat impossible."*

Mental toughness is a form of positioning. A gritty team keeps going where others quit.

1.3 Clarity: The Antidote to Chaos

When goals are vague and roles are unclear, teams collapse into confusion. Clarity removes friction and doubt.

Clarify:

- Who owns what

- What success looks like

- How priorities are chosen

> *"If words of command are not clear and distinct, if orders are not thoroughly understood, the general is to blame."*

The founder's first duty is clarity—**not charisma**.

---

2. Leading in Uncertainty and Crisis

> *"In the midst of chaos, there is also opportunity."*

You will face a moment—likely many—when everything feels like it's breaking. Cash is low. A key hire leaves. A product flops. What you do next determines whether your team rallies or dissolves.

2.1 Be the Eye of the Storm

Your team takes its emotional cues from you. If you're panicked, they'll crumble. If you're calm, they'll adapt.

In a crisis:

- Speak simply. Avoid jargon or spin.

- Be brutally honest about the challenge—but clear about the plan.

- Use rhythm (daily standups, crisis briefings) to stabilize the team.

"The wise warrior avoids the battle."

You can't avoid every crisis, but you can avoid **self-created ones** by staying composed.

2.2 Decisiveness as a Leadership Trait

The worst thing in a crisis is indecision. You don't need to be right every time. But you must move.

"Let your plans be dark and impenetrable as night,
and when you move, fall like a thunderbolt."

People want leaders who **decide with conviction**, even in ambiguity. Make a call. Communicate it. Own the outcome.

2.3 Psychological Safety in the Trenches

Teams in chaos need to feel safe bringing problems forward. That requires a culture of candor without punishment.

Tactics:

- Never shoot the messenger

- Reward problem-spotters, not just problem-solvers

- Publicly acknowledge uncertainty—but also outline paths forward

> *"The general who advances without coveting fame and retreats without fearing disgrace... is the jewel of the kingdom."*

Let your team feel like soldiers in service of something bigger—not cogs in a panic machine.

---

3. Aligning Incentives and Giving Your Team a Mission

> *"Unite the troops under a single standard to bring them together."*

People will go to war for many reasons—but they stay in it for few: purpose, pride, and payoff. As a founder, you are responsible for all three.

3.1 Align Incentives to Outcomes

If compensation and career growth aren't linked to real success, your team will game the system—or quit.

Tactical alignment tips:

- Link OKRs to bonuses or recognition

- Set clear, fair equity expectations (and explain the long-term upside)

- Make it visible who's moving the needle

> *"If rewards are beyond reach, the troops lose interest."*

Don't just promise upside. Show the **path to it**.

3.2 Define a Mission Worth Following

Not "we make software." Not "we're a SaaS company." A real mission has teeth. It's something people are proud to tell their families about.

Examples:

- "We help teachers spend less time on paperwork so they can spend more time with kids."

- "We're creating the infrastructure for a carbon-negative economy."

"Treat your men as you would your own beloved sons, and they will follow you into the deepest valley."

Give your people a reason to care **beyond survival**.

3.3 Build Rituals That Reinforce Mission

Culture is kept alive by repetition. Make the mission **part of how you operate**, not just what's printed on the wall.

Examples:

- "Customer Stories Fridays": team hears directly from a user

- Quarterly retros with stories of mission impact

- Hiring process includes storytelling about why the company exists

"When the outlook is bright, bring it before their eyes; but tell them nothing when the situation is gloomy."

Control the emotional rhythm. Use ritual to keep morale anchored.

---

4. Action: Culture Codex + Leadership Audit

Culture must be defined **deliberately**. And leadership must be evaluated **consistently**. These tools help you do both.

Part 1: Culture Codex

Write this down. Share it. Live it.

1. Core Values (3–5 max)

- What do we believe?

- What behaviors do we reward?

- What do we never tolerate?

2. How We Work

- How decisions are made

- How feedback is delivered

- What our weekly rhythm looks like

3. What We Fight For

- Who is our customer?

- What world are we trying to build?

- Why does it matter?

Part 2: Leadership Audit (Do Quarterly)

1. Self-Awareness

- Do I model the behavior I expect?

- Do I accept feedback with openness?

2. Clarity

- Are my team's goals clear?

- Are roles and responsibilities understood?

3. Trust

- Do I give my team autonomy?

- Do they feel safe raising concerns?

4. Communication

- Do I say what needs to be said?

- Do I listen without judgment?

5. Cadence

- Do we have consistent rituals?

- Are we building or just reacting?

"Leadership is a matter of intelligence, trustworthiness, humaneness, courage, and sternness."

You don't need to be perfect. But you do need to be honest—with yourself first.

Conclusion: Lead Like a General, Serve Like a Guardian

"When he treats his soldiers like his own beloved children, they will die with him."

Sun Tzu didn't believe in control through fear. He believed in control through **loyalty**. Through shared danger, shared goals, and shared discipline.

Your job is not just to lead. It's to **build leaders**.
 Not just to inspire—but to enforce focus.
 Not just to serve the mission—but to remind people why it matters.

The best startup leaders don't just command loyalty. They **earn it**—day after day, battle after battle.

So ask yourself:

- Am I modeling the behavior I want repeated?

- Have I given my team something worth fighting for?

- Do they feel seen, challenged, protected?

If so, you're not just building a company.
 You're building an army.

And when that army is bound by trust, grit, and mission—

"They will follow you into the deepest valleys."

Chapter 9: Adapt or Die

"Water shapes its course according to the nature of the ground over which it flows." – Sun Tzu

---

Introduction: The Startup That Can't Adapt Is Already Dead

In war, no plan survives contact with the enemy. In startups, no business model survives contact with reality. Market shifts, user behavior changes, technology evolves, and assumptions break. The founders who thrive are not the ones with the most perfect vision, but those who can **pivot with precision**.

Sun Tzu understood this deeply. His metaphor of water—fluid, responsive, always seeking the path of least resistance—is a perfect description of what modern startups must become.

> *"Water shapes its course according to the nature of the ground over which it flows; the soldier works out his victory in relation to the foe whom he is facing."*

Adaptation is not weakness. It's mastery. This chapter explores:

- The art and discipline of pivoting

- How to build continuous feedback loops

- Case studies of smart and fatal pivots

- A tactical tool: Pivot Checklist + Adaptability Scorecard

---

1. Pivoting With Precision: When, How, and Why

"When you surround an army, leave an outlet. Do not press a desperate foe too hard."

The pivot is your outlet. It's your strategic maneuver, not your admission of failure. But a pivot done wrong is just flailing.

1.1 What Is a Pivot (Really)?

A pivot is a structured shift in one or more of the following:

- **Customer**: serving a different audience

- **Problem**: solving a new pain point

- **Solution**: building a different product

- **Channel**: changing how you reach or monetize

- **Model**: altering your business fundamentals

A pivot is **not** a panic move. It's a **calculated adaptation** based on data, not desperation.

1.2 When to Pivot

"If quick, I survive. If not quick, I am lost."

Timing is everything. Wait too long, and you burn cash and team morale. Pivot too early, and you might miss latent traction.

Signals it's time:

- Your users love your mission, not your product

- Core metrics are flat despite iteration

- The market reality has changed (tech, policy, competitors)

- You've validated a better opportunity than your current path

Gut check question:
If you had to start the company again tomorrow, would you build what you're building now?

If not—it's time to reassess.

1.3 How to Pivot Without Breaking Everything

Pivots should be clear, fast, and emotionally managed. Teams fear change when it feels reactive. You must turn the pivot into a strategy, not a scramble.

Steps:

1. Validate the new direction with minimal resources

2. Communicate the "why" with full honesty to your team

3. Retire or sunset previous efforts respectfully

4. Retain your best learnings—don't start from zero

> *"Move not unless you see an advantage; use not your troops unless there is something to be gained."*

Pivoting is a resource-intensive play. **Do it because the ground has shifted—not because you're bored.**

---

2. Continuous Feedback Loops With Customers

> *"He who exercises no forethought but makes light of his opponents is sure to be captured by them."*

Every day you operate without listening to customers, you drift from truth. Startups must be **machines for learning**, not just machines for building.

2.1 Build Feedback Into the Core Loop

Don't wait until launch. Don't wait for support tickets. Build a culture and system of **ongoing feedback**.

Tactics:

- Embed "How was this experience?" micro-surveys inside the product

- Regularly email active users for 10-minute feedback calls

- Assign product managers to own "voice of the customer" meetings monthly

> *"Know the enemy and know yourself, and you can fight a hundred battles without disaster."*

Your users are not your enemy—but ignorance of their needs **is**.

2.2 Ask Better Questions

Stop asking "Do you like it?" or "Would you use this?" Ask:

- "What do you do today instead?"

- "What almost stopped you from signing up?"

- "When was the last time you felt this problem most painfully?"

The goal is **truth**, not compliments.

> *"All warfare is based on deception."*

But you should deceive no one—especially not yourself. Flattery is the enemy of adaptation.

2.3 Feedback Isn't a Feature Request Log

It's not about building everything users ask for. It's about **interpreting the pain** behind their asks.

Build what matters. Ignore what doesn't. Create signal-processing systems to filter:

- What's repeated?

- What's urgent?

- What maps to your vision?

Then adapt accordingly.

> *"When you are ignorant of the enemy but know yourself, your chances of winning or losing are equal."*

Customer feedback turns guessing into knowing.

3. Case Studies: Successful and Failed Pivots

Let's examine how smart adaptation led to massive success—and how rigidity led to collapse.

3.1 Successful Pivot: Slack

Original idea: Online multiplayer game
Pivot: Internal communication tool used during development
Why it worked:

- Clear pain point: scattered team comms

- Early adoption inside other startups

- Strong narrative around productivity and delight

Slack became the fastest-growing B2B SaaS ever. The pivot wasn't random—it was built on **internal feedback**, **validated use**, and **clarity of value**.

> *"Opportunities multiply as they are seized."*

Slack didn't just pivot once. They iterated again and again, from freemium pricing to integrations and channel architecture.

3.2 Successful Pivot: Instagram

Original idea: Burbn—a location-based check-in app with photo
features
 Pivot: Stripped away everything but photo sharing
 Why it worked:

- Users loved the photo filters

- Check-ins were noise

- Focus created traction

By simplifying the app, Instagram unlocked explosive daily usage.

> *"Let your plans be dark and impenetrable as night,*
> *and when you move, fall like a thunderbolt."*

The shift was quiet—until the growth was loud.

3.3 Failed Pivot: Quibi

Original idea: Mobile-only short-form premium video content
 Pivot: None—despite market signals
 Why it failed:

- Ignored user behavior trends (multi-device usage)

- Launched mid-pandemic when commutes vanished

- Refused to license content to other platforms

They clung to their vision while the world changed.

> *"A kingdom that has once been destroyed can never come again into being."*

Startups are fragile kingdoms. Refuse to pivot, and they vanish.

---

4. Action: Pivot Checklist + Adaptability Scorecard

You don't need to guess when it's time to adapt. You need a framework to decide, and a tool to measure how ready you are.

Pivot Checklist: When to Pull the Trigger

1. **Are users engaging deeply?**

   - If churn is high and usage is shallow, reconsider your approach.

2. **Have core metrics flatlined?**

   - Repeated cycles without growth = strategic misalignment.

3. **Is the original market smaller than expected?**

- Shrinking TAM = rethink your problem or audience.

4. **Is there stronger pull elsewhere?**

    - A surprising side feature getting traction? That's a wedge.

5. **Would you build this again from scratch?**

    - If the answer is no, it's time.

"Do not repeat the tactics which have gained you one victory, but let your methods be regulated by the infinite variety of circumstances."

What worked before may not work now.

Adaptability Scorecard: Grade Your Startup

Rate yourself from 1 (low) to 5 (high):

Factor	Score (1–5)	Notes
Team openness to change		
Speed of feedback loops		
Frequency of experiments		

Leadership humility

User insight depth

Willingness to sunset
products

Ability to test new models

Interpretation:

- 30–35: Elite adaptability

- 20–29: Capable, but cautious

- Below 20: At risk of stagnation

> *"If you know both yourself and your enemy, you will not be imperiled in a hundred battles."*

This scorecard helps you know **yourself**—and prepares you to adjust to anything.

Conclusion: Be Like Water, Or Be Forgotten

> *"Just as water retains no constant shape, so in warfare there are no constant conditions."*

No startup ever scales exactly as planned. Those that win do so by flowing **around resistance**, not trying to break through it.

- They listen harder than others.

- They test faster than others.

- They kill their darlings quicker than others.

Adaptation is not a fallback—it's a superpower. In Sun Tzu's world, water is the metaphor for survival and success. It's flexible, fluid, relentless. Be water.

So ask yourself:

- Are you clinging to a dead plan?

- Are you listening to signals or justifying old decisions?

- Are you building a company, or defending an ego?

Your answer determines your fate.

Because in war, as in startups—

"Adapt or die."

Chapter 10: Victory Without Complacency

"In war, let your great object be victory, not lengthy campaigns." – Sun Tzu

---

Introduction: The Battle Isn't Over—It Just Changes

Success is a seductive trap. When you finally achieve product-market fit, raise a major round, or hit profitability, you've won a critical battle. But if you let that moment seduce you into relaxation, comfort, or overconfidence—**you've already begun to lose.**

Sun Tzu, who preached the virtues of patience and precision, warned against prolonged, unfocused wars. **Victory must be decisive.** It must be won with purpose—and followed by restraint.

> *"In war, then, let your great object be victory, not lengthy campaigns."*

Startups that drag themselves into endless growth without strategy suffer from bloat, burnout, and drift. This chapter is about how to win—and keep winning—without losing your discipline.

We'll cover:

- How to stay focused after success

- How to prevent bloat and avoid distraction

- How to build discipline into the post-launch phase

- How to set up systems for long-term strength

- A tactical framework: The 3-Year War Plan + Post-Launch Discipline Tracker

---

1. Winning with Focus: Avoid Bloat, Drift, and Distraction

"There is no instance of a country having benefited from prolonged warfare."

Many founders operate like they're still fighting the first war long after they've won it. Instead of consolidating gains, they **expand too fast**, build too much, and try to do everything.

Success requires focus just as much as the early grind did. Maybe even more.

1.1 The Temptation of Bloat

Once success hits, the team grows. Resources grow. Expectations explode. You finally have freedom—and that freedom can become your downfall.

Common signs of post-success bloat:

- Shipping features that don't serve your core users

- Hiring departments without a clear plan

- Creating projects to justify headcount

> *"The wise general makes a point of foraging on the enemy."*

Translation: Use what you've won wisely. Grow by leveraging your advantages—not by overextending.

1.2 The Danger of Strategic Drift

When you try to pursue every opportunity, you end up pursuing **none effectively**. Focus is what got you here. Focus is what keeps you here.

Tactical signals of drift:

- KPIs balloon from 3 to 15

- Your mission statement gets revised every six months

- You're serving customer segments you don't even understand

"He will win who has military capacity and is not interfered with by the sovereign."

In startups, "the sovereign" is often your own ego—or the noise of your boardroom. If you're pulled in too many directions, you become unstrategic.

1.3 Avoiding Distraction Through Clear Strategy

To stay focused, set a single North Star Metric—and **revisit it weekly**. Every initiative should ladder up to that outcome.

Ask:

- Is this project moving the needle?

- Is it distracting us from our mission?

- Can we win bigger by doing less?

"Speed is the essence of war."

Don't confuse motion for progress. Focus speeds everything up. Distraction kills momentum.

---

2. Post-Success Discipline: Guarding Against Hubris

*"He who exercises no forethought but makes light of
his opponents is sure to be captured by them."*

Success creates a false sense of invincibility. When things go well, it's easy to stop listening, stop questioning, and stop pushing.

The greatest companies in history were undone **not by failure—but by complacency.**

2.1 Hubris Is the Silent Killer

Hubris shows up as:

- Ignoring negative signals from the market

- Dismissing customer complaints because "we know better"

- Assuming the brand will carry new products without effort

*"When envoys are sent with compliments in their
mouths, it is a sign that the enemy wishes for a truce."*

Flattery from the market is often a prelude to decline. Don't mistake applause for security.

2.2 Run Post-Win Postmortems

After every major success—launch, fundraise, acquisition—run a retro. Ask:

- What worked because of luck?

- What could have failed but didn't?

- Where did we get sloppy under pressure?

Success should create **self-awareness**, not self-congratulation.

> *"Plan for what is difficult while it is easy, do what is great while it is small."*

When things are going well, plan for turbulence.

2.3 Maintain a Challenger Mindset

Never act like the incumbent—even when you become one. Keep the hunger alive by:

- Setting bold stretch goals

- Running internal sprints with external deadlines

- Giving small, focused teams autonomy to build like insurgents

> *"When the outlook is bright, bring it before their eyes;
> but tell them nothing when the situation is gloomy."*

Celebrate wins—but only as fuel for the next battle.

---

3. Building Long-Term Resilience and Systems

> *"Therefore, just as water retains no constant shape,
> so in warfare there are no constant conditions."*

Victory is a moment. Resilience is what sustains it.

After product-market fit, your job is to build **systems**—not just culture. Systems for hiring. Systems for scaling. Systems for decision-making and accountability.

3.1 Operationalize Success

What used to happen organically now needs **structure**. You can't rely on hustle forever.

Core systems to install:

- Weekly OKR check-ins

- Data dashboards for each department

- Rituals for leadership decision-making

Resilience means planning for shocks before they hit.

3.2 Build Anti-Fragility Into the Org

An antifragile company **gets stronger under stress**. That means testing your systems and your people before the real test arrives.

Tactics:

- Run "chaos drills" to simulate crisis scenarios

- Rotate team leads on short, high-stakes projects

- Cross-train roles to reduce single points of failure

Wait—but not passively. Prepare yourself while your competitors sleep.

3.3 Create a Culture of Learning, Not Legacy

Resilient companies keep learning. That means:

- Sharing learnings from failed experiments publicly

- Rewarding people for intelligent risk-taking

- Encouraging questions over unquestioned habits

> *"Do not repeat the tactics which have gained you one victory."*

Systems must evolve with the company. Don't let yesterday's playbook become today's prison.

---

4. Action: 3-Year War Plan + Post-Launch Discipline Tracker

> *"To win one hundred victories in one hundred battles is not the acme of skill. To subdue the enemy without fighting is the acme of skill."*

You must think and plan like a general. Here's how.

Part 1: 3-Year War Plan

This isn't just a roadmap—it's your strategy for continued dominance.

1. Strategic Objective (Year 3)

- Where do you want the company to be?

- What would make you defensible, desirable, and durable?

2. Year 1 Objectives

- Consolidate core market

- Reinforce product strength

- Strengthen operations and hiring

3. Year 2 Objectives

- Expand into adjacent segments

- Launch new monetization layers

- Grow brand authority and ecosystem

4. Year 3 Objectives

- Platformize or productize internal systems

- Open strategic partnerships or M&A

- Operational excellence across all units

"Victorious warriors win first and then go to war."

Plan the win. Then move.

Part 2: Post-Launch Discipline Tracker
Use this every week to guard against post-launch chaos and keep your venture on course. Share and review these checkpoints with your leadership team—anything flagged Red demands immediate action.

1. Strategic Focus

- *Current Status:* (Green / Yellow / Red)

- *Notes:* How well are you sticking to your core priorities? Highlight any emerging distractions or new opportunities that might pull you off course.

2. Execution Rhythm

- *Current Status:* (Green / Yellow / Red)

- *Notes:* Are sprints, milestones, and deliverables landing on schedule? Identify bottlenecks slowing delivery or process breakdowns that need fixing.

3. Metrics Clarity

- *Current Status:* (Green / Yellow / Red)

- *Notes:* Do teams have clear KPIs, dashboards, and reporting rhythms? Call out any ambiguous or conflicting data streams that are undermining decision-making.

---

4. Team Morale

- *Current Status:* (Green / Yellow / Red)

- *Notes:* Assess sentiment through pulse surveys, 1:1s, and anecdotal feedback. Flag any frustration, burnout, or misalignment that requires leadership attention.

---

5. Customer Feedback Loops

- *Current Status:* (Green / Yellow / Red)

- *Notes:* Are support tickets, NPS scores, and in-app suggestions flowing into product and service improvements? Highlight gaps in responsiveness or patterns of dissatisfaction.

---

6. Experimentation Cadence

- *Current Status:* (Green / Yellow / Red)

- *Notes:* Is your innovation engine still running? Track the number of active experiments, their success rates, and any lulls in new idea generation.

Weekly Review Protocol
 Gather your executive team each week to update these six areas. Green means stay the course; Yellow signals caution and potential adjustments; Red indicates a pressing issue—assign owners, define remedies, and set firm deadlines to move back to Yellow or Green.

esn't mean failure—it means **you still have an enemy to face.**

Conclusion: Win the War, Then Keep the Peace

"He who wishes to fight must first count the cost."

Every win comes with a cost—burnout, complexity, ego. Real mastery is knowing how to stay strong **after the war is won.**

- Focus keeps you dangerous

- Discipline keeps you sharp

- Systems keep you strong

- And clarity keeps you from wandering

> *"In war, let your great object be victory, not lengthy campaigns."*

Startup life is not meant to be a series of endless battles. Win fast. Consolidate smart. Grow wisely.

Victory is not a license to relax.
It's a responsibility to stay ready.

So ask yourself:

- Are we still focused?

- Are we still listening?

- Are we still preparing for the next campaign?

Because when your team is sharp, your system is tight, and your eyes are on the next hill—

You win without dragging yourself into a war you don't need to fight.

That's how you win the battle—and keep the peace.

Conclusion: The War Never Ends—And That's the Point

"The skillful fighter puts himself into a position which makes defeat impossible, and does not miss the moment for defeating the enemy." – Sun Tzu

---

Introduction: Beyond Victory—Into Vigilance

A founder's journey is not a single war, but a series of campaigns. Each milestone—funding, product-market fit, scale, profitability—is a battle won. But there is no endgame. There is only what comes next.

Sun Tzu teaches us that **strategy is not a checklist.** It's a way of seeing. A way of sensing. A way of navigating. And in that light, entrepreneurship is not a sprint, or even a marathon—it is a kind of warfare. Quiet, creative, relentless.

The war never ends—not because the world is cruel, but because the world **keeps moving**. So must you.

This chapter explores:

- Strategy as a mindset, not a manual

- Staying sharp in both peacetime and conflict

- Why every entrepreneur is, in fact, a general in disguise

---

1. Strategy as a Way of Thinking, Not a Set of Rules

"The whole secret lies in confusing the enemy, so that he cannot fathom our real intent."

Rules are brittle. Playbooks get outdated. Markets shift. Competitors adapt. That's why strategy must live in the mind—not just in the manual.

1.1 Static Plans Don't Survive Dynamic Environments

No business survives exactly as its pitch deck predicted. And no strategy—no matter how brilliant—survives without adaptation.

"Just as water retains no constant shape, so in warfare there are no constant conditions."

What does survive?

- Mental flexibility

- Constant learning

- Awareness of terrain, timing, and movement

Strategy is about **how you think when the ground shifts**, not how you act when it's stable.

1.2 Real Strategy Is About Choices

It's not about doing everything right. It's about choosing **what not to do.** It's about **focus**, **sequencing**, and **sacrifice**.

> *"He who wishes to fight must first count the cost."*

Strategic thinking means saying no to:

- Features that dilute your vision

- Customers that don't align

- Short-term wins that sabotage long-term position

If you chase everything, you win nothing.

1.3 Principles Over Playbooks

Instead of rigid methods, great generals—and great founders—build **mental models** based on timeless principles:

- Understand the terrain

- Attack weakness, not strength

- Move quickly and decisively

- Deceive with confidence

- Lead with clarity

These are not startup hacks. They are truths about conflict, power, and movement. They are as relevant in 500 BC as in your next investor meeting.

> *"The general who wins a battle makes many calculations in his temple before the battle is fought."*

Build your temple. Make your calculations. And remember—strategy is not what you do. It's how you think.

---

2. Staying Sharp in Peace and Conflict

> *"The victorious army first obtains conditions for victory, then engages in battle."*

Startups are forged in chaos, but scaled in calm. And that's the trap. In the quiet moments, founders grow soft. They stop preparing. They lose their edge.

Sun Tzu taught us: **peace is the time for preparation.** Conflict is just the reveal.

2.1 Don't Wait for Pressure to Be Proactive

The best generals drill when others rest. They sharpen tools when others celebrate. They assume danger even when surrounded by praise.

> *"If you know the enemy and know yourself, you need not fear the result of a hundred battles."*

Knowing yourself means being honest about:

- Where your company is fragile

- What your blind spots are

- Which people, systems, or assumptions won't scale

Use peacetime to audit the foundations. Harden your systems. Tighten your strategy.

2.2 Build Systems That Survive You

If your startup can't operate without you—it's not a company. It's a cult of personality. Great founders **embed their thinking into the culture,** not just the meetings.

> *"If orders are not thoroughly understood, the general is to blame."*

Create:

- A living strategy document

- Clear decision-making frameworks

- Embedded rituals that reinforce focus and speed

This is how you make your company not just **successful**, but **self-sustaining.**

2.3 Run Peace Drills Like War Games

Don't wait for a crisis to test your resilience.

Try this:

- Simulate a customer churn spike—what do you do?

- Cut your burn by 30% in a mock drill—how do you decide?

- Lose your top engineer—who's cross-trained?

> *"When you are near, make it appear that you are far away; when far away, that you are near."*

Train for surprise. Prepare for betrayal. Strength is built when it's least needed—so it's available when it matters most.

3. Every Entrepreneur Is a General in Disguise

> *"Leadership is a matter of intelligence, trustworthiness, humaneness, courage, and sternness."*

Founders aren't just builders. They're generals—whether they realize it or not. They're leading troops, drawing maps, choosing terrain, negotiating truces, setting traps, and declaring war.

To be a great founder, you must master the mindset of a commander.

3.1 Intelligence: Know More Than the Map

Sun Tzu valued intelligence above tactics. Founders must do the same.

> *"If you know the terrain and know the weather, your victory will then be total."*

You must study:

- Customer behavior and psychology

- Competitor positioning and weaknesses

- Market forces and timing cues

- Internal culture and execution patterns

Strategy isn't something you "set." It's something you **study and adapt** every day.

3.2 Trustworthiness: Build Loyalty That Outlasts Paychecks

People don't follow charisma. They follow consistency.

> *"Treat your men as you would your own beloved sons, and they will follow you into the deepest valley."*

Be the kind of founder who:

- Does what they say

- Protects their team during storms

- Shares both credit and blame

- Sets standards and lives by them

That loyalty will be your most underpriced asset in tough times.

3.3 Humaneness: Lead with Empathy, Not Ego

Empathy isn't weakness—it's leverage. Knowing how your team feels is how you unlock real effort.

- Listen before you decide

- Ask how decisions affect real lives

- Create space for challenge and disagreement

> *"When you lay down a rule, begin by enforcing it with iron discipline; then, when your soldiers have grown used to it, you can relax the severity."*

Earn the right to ease up. But only after the standards are burned into the culture.

3.4 Courage and Sternness: Make Hard Calls Fast

Startup leadership is a chain of tough decisions. When to cut. When to fire. When to pivot. When to say no to a shiny opportunity.

> *"He who is prudent and lies in wait for an enemy who is not, will be victorious."*

Be brave enough to wait. And bold enough to strike.

The general who can't kill a bad idea—or enforce the mission—is not a general. They're a mascot.

---

4. The Next Battle Is Already on the Horizon

> *"He will win who knows how to handle both superior and inferior forces."*

Right now, there's a team out there with less funding, fewer employees, and more fire. They're watching you. Studying your weaknesses. Waiting for your blind spot.

You were once them. Hungry. Focused. Scrappy.

Now you're the one with something to lose.

This isn't paranoia—it's reality. And it's your motivation to stay sharp.

- Reinvent before you need to

- Question what no longer serves you

- Fire the idea, not the team

- Win without ego, scale without drift

> *"A wise general makes a point of foraging on the enemy."*

Look at your competitors for leverage, not fear. Learn from them. Out-think them. Outspeed them.

Victory is not a trophy. It's a position. And that position is always under threat.

---

5. Strategy Never Ends—And That's the Point

"Therefore the skillful leader subdues the enemy's troops without any fighting; he captures their cities without laying siege; he overthrows their kingdom without lengthy operations in the field."

This is what modern entrepreneurship demands: subtlety, speed, patience, presence.

There will always be:

- New battles (emerging competitors, shifting regulations)

- Internal chaos (misalignment, ego, burnout)

- False victories (vanity metrics, short-term wins)

And you? You are the one responsible for keeping your company **ready for the next campaign**.

Because the war never ends. Not if you're doing it right.

That's not a burden. It's an opportunity.

It means:

- You keep learning

- You keep evolving

- You never coast

- You never stop mastering the craft

> *"Victorious warriors win first and then go to war, while defeated warriors go to war first and then seek to win."*

You win every day, in the small decisions. In the discipline. In the focus. In the grit.

Final Thoughts: The Founder as Field Commander

You started as a maker. A hacker. A builder.

But now, you're a general. Not because you declared it—but because the role demanded it.

You are:

- The mind behind the movement

- The spirit behind the culture

- The sword behind the decisions

- The shield in the storm

And if you understand the terrain, command with clarity, listen like a spy, and strike like a hawk—**you'll not only win battles. You'll keep winning them.**

So here is your final order:

Stay sharp.
Stay fast.
Stay fluid.
Stay dangerous.

> *"The war never ends—and that's the point."*

Because in that endless battle lies your real edge.

Not the tools.
Not the tactics.
But the mindset.

THIS IS NOT A COLLECTION

This volume is part of **Ancient Wisdom Hacks**—
an ongoing body of work focused on how strategy, power, and
failure actually function under pressure.

The books are only one layer.

What you are reading is an entry point into a larger system of
interpretation, application, and expansion.

WHAT THESE WORKS ARE DESIGNED TO DO

Most people look for answers.

These works expose patterns:

- How decisions are made before they are visible
- How systems weaken before they collapse
- How power shifts before it is recognized

This is not theory.
It is applied observation.

THE SYSTEM BEHIND THE WORK

Across all volumes and future releases, three forces remain
constant:

- **Strategy** — how outcomes are shaped before action
- **Conflict** — how people and systems break under pressure
- **Power** — how control is gained, maintained, and lost

No single book contains the full picture.
Each adds another angle.

CONTINUE BEYOND THIS VOLUME

New interpretations, applied volumes, and extended works are
released continuously.

To access current and future material, visit:

www.AncientWisdomHacks.com

WHAT YOU WILL FIND

- Additional applied volumes across industries
- Expanded interpretations of foundational texts
- New releases not available through standard distribution
- Future projects extending beyond books

The system is still expanding.

FINAL POSITION

Clarity does not make outcomes easier.

It removes the illusion that they were ever simple.

Ancient Wisdom Hacks
Interpretation over repetition.
Application over theory.